M000308867

Little Lessons from
St. Thérèse of Lisieux

Copyright © 2015 by Gracewatch Media. All rights reserved.

Artwork copyright © 2015 by Jeanine Crowe.
All rights reserved.

No part of this book may be reproduced by any means
without the written permission of the publisher.

Printed in the United States of America

First Edition: December 2015

ISBN 978-1-944008-10-9

Gracewatch Media
Winona, Minnesota
www.gracewatch.org

 gracewatch.media

Little Lessons from St. Thérèse of Lisieux

An Introduction to Her Words and Wisdom

Thérèse of Lisieux

text selected and adapted by Becky Arganbright

illustrated by Jeanine Crowe

Gracewatch Media
Winona, Minnesota

A brief introduction to St. Thérèse

Once upon a time, there was a young woman named Thérèse Martin who wanted to give her whole self to Jesus. She wanted to "accomplish the most heroic deeds" for him; she wanted to be a saint, a prophet, a martyr, a Doctor of the Church, a missionary.

"I would be a light unto souls; I would travel to every land to preach Your name, O my Beloved. . . . I would spread the Gospel to the ends of the earth, even to the most distant isles."

Thérèse Martin eventually accomplished all of those things—although not in the way she might have imagined. In 1888, at the age of fifteen, she joined a small community of Carmelite sisters in Lisieux, France. The community was cloistered, meaning the nuns never left the convent where they lived. She passed nine quiet years there before dying of tuberculosis at the young age of twenty-four.

To the outside world, it might have seemed that Thérèse failed to realize any of her dreams. Yet her Carmelite sisters knew better. They were so impressed with her way of life that the Mother Superior commanded her to write down the story of her life, along with all of her thoughts.

The resulting book, *Story of a Soul*, explained how anyone might do great things for Jesus simply by depending entirely on him, much as a little child depends on a grownup for help; she called this her "little way."

In the years since her death in 1897, the book has been read by millions of people. The words of the young woman who called herself "little Thérèse" brought the light of Jesus to every land in the world. Today, the Church honors her not only as a saint, but as a patron of missionaries and a Doctor of the Church (one of the Church's greatest teachers).

If you would like to do great things for Jesus too, then maybe you will find help and inspiration from the words of St. Thérèse contained in the following pages. These selections from *Story of a Soul* were chosen to provide a brief introduction to some of the essential themes of her spirituality. These short readings are accompanied by the artwork of award-winning watercolorist Jeanine Crowe as an aid to prayerful meditation on the words and wisdom of the saint.

St. Thérèse is "a companionable presence…joyful, patient, and generous," says Father James Martin, S.J., one of her many admirers. "She is someone whose company, had I known her [from an earlier age], would have made me a better Christian."

Through her words on these pages, may you come to know her in the same way, and through her, the abundant love of Christ.

Sing of God's goodness

Now, like a flower after the storm, I can raise my head and see that the words of the Psalm are realized in me: "The Lord is my Shepherd and I shall want nothing...."

And so it gives me great joy to sing His unspeakable mercies.

If a little flower could speak, it seems to me that it would tell us quite simply all that God has done for it, without hiding any of its gifts. It would not, under the pretext of humility, say that it was not pretty, or that it had not a sweet scent, that the sun had withered its petals, or the storm bruised its stem, if it knew that such were not the case.

The Little Flower, that now tells her tale, rejoiced in having to write the wholly undeserved favors bestowed upon her by Our Lord. She knows that she had nothing in herself worthy of attracting Him: His Mercy alone showered blessings on her.

Acknowledge that all comes from God

God has loaded my soul with graces for me and for many others. And it is my dearest wish ever to bend beneath the weight of God's gifts, acknowledging that all comes from Him.

Bind yourself more closely to Jesus

If you wish to be a Saint—and it will not be hard—keep only one end in view: make Jesus happy and bind yourself more closely to Him.

Open the Holy Gospels

As Our Lord is now in Heaven, I can only follow Him by the footprints He has left—footprints full of life, full of fragrance. I have only to open the Holy Gospels and at once I breathe the perfume of Jesus, and then I know which way to run; and it is not to the first place, but to the last, that I hasten.

To love God alone

My God, You know that I have always desired to love You alone. It has been my only ambition. Your love has gone before me, even from the days of my childhood. It has grown with my growth, and now it is an abyss whose depths I cannot fathom.

Love attracts love; mine darts towards You, and would gladly make the abyss brim over, but alas! it is not even as a dewdrop in the ocean. To love You as You love me, I must make Your Love my own. Thus alone can I find rest.

I lift up my heart to God in trust and love

It is not because I have been preserved from mortal sin that I lift up my heart to God in trust and love. I feel that even had I on my conscience every crime one could commit, I should lose nothing of my confidence: my heart broken with sorrow, I would throw myself into the Arms of my Savior. I know that He loves the Prodigal Son, I have heard His words to St. Mary Magdalen, to the woman taken in adultery, and to the woman of Samaria. No one could frighten me, for I know what to believe concerning His Mercy and His Love. And I know that all that multitude of sins would disappear in an instant, even as a drop of water cast into a flaming furnace.

Getting to Heaven by a little way

You know it has ever been my desire to become a Saint, but I have always felt, in comparing myself with the Saints, that I am as far removed from them as the grain of sand, which the passer-by tramples underfoot, is remote from the mountain whose summit is lost in the clouds.

Instead of being discouraged, I concluded that God would not inspire desires which could not be realized, and that I may aspire to holiness in spite of my littleness. For me to become great is impossible. I must bear with myself and my many imperfections; but I will seek out a means of getting to Heaven by a little way— very short and very straight, a little way that is wholly new.

We live in an age of inventions; nowadays the rich need not trouble to climb the stairs; they have elevators instead. Well, I mean to try and find an elevator by which I may be raised unto God, for I am too tiny to climb the steep stairway of perfection. I have sought to find in Holy Scripture some suggestion as to what this elevator might be which I so much desired, and I read these words uttered by the Eternal Wisdom Itself: "Whosoever is a little one, let him come to Me."

Then I drew near to God, feeling sure that I had discovered what I sought; but wishing to know further what He would do to the little one, I continued my search and this is what I found: "You shall be carried at the breasts and upon the knees; as one whom the mother caresses, so will I comfort you."

Never have I been consoled by words more tender and sweet. Your Arms, then, O Jesus, are the elevator which must raise me up even unto Heaven. To get there I need not grow; on the contrary, I must remain little, I must become still less. O my God, you have gone beyond my expectation, and I… "I will sing Your mercies! You have taught me, O Lord, from my youth and till now I have declared Your wonderful works…."

Remain always very little

The only way to advance rapidly in the path of love is to remain always very little. That is what I did, and now I can sing with our holy Father, St. John of the Cross:

> *Then I abased myself so low, so very low,*
> *That I ascended to such heights, such heights indeed,*
> *That I did overtake the prey I chased!*

Await everything from the Goodness of God

"Remaining little" means to recognize one's nothingness, to await everything from the Goodness of God, to avoid being too much troubled at our faults; finally, not to worry over amassing spiritual riches, not to be solicitous about anything. Even among the poor, while a child is still small, he is given what is necessary; but, once he is grown up, his father will no longer feed him, and tells him to seek work and support himself. Well, it was to avoid hearing this, that I have never wished to grow up, for I feel incapable of earning my livelihood, which is Life Eternal!

My way is the way of spiritual childhood, the way of trust and absolute self-surrender.

The nearer one approaches
God, the simpler one becomes.

God will carry you

You make me think of a little child that is learning to stand but does not yet know how to walk. In his desire to reach the top of the stairs to find his mother, he lifts his little foot to climb the first step. It is all in vain, and at each renewed effort he falls. Well, be like that little child. Always keep lifting your foot to climb the ladder of holiness, and do not imagine that you can mount even the first step. All God asks of you is good will. From the top of the ladder He looks lovingly upon you, and soon, touched by your fruitless efforts, He will Himself come down, and, taking you in His Arms, will carry you to His Kingdom never again to leave Him. But should you cease to raise your foot, you will be left for long on the earth.

Prayer is an uplifting of the heart

How wonderful is the power of prayer! It is like a queen, who, having free access to the king, obtains whatsoever she asks. In order to secure a hearing there is no need to recite set prayers… were it so, I ought indeed to be pitied! … I have not the courage to look through books for beautiful prayers. I only get a headache because of their number, and besides, one is more lovely than another. Unable therefore to say them all, and lost in choice, I do as children who have not learned to read—I simply tell Our Lord all that I want, and He always understands.

With me prayer is an uplifting of the heart; a glance towards heaven; a cry of gratitude and love, uttered equally in sorrow and in joy. In a word, it is something noble, supernatural, which expands my soul and unites it to God. Sometimes when I am in such a state of spiritual dryness that not a single good thought occurs to me, I say very slowly the "Our Father" or the "Hail Mary," and these prayers suffice to take me out of myself, and wonderfully refresh me.

Sacrifices and acts of love

I shall always remember my First Communion Day as one of unclouded happiness. It seems to me that I could not have been better prepared.... Each day I made a number of little sacrifices and acts of love, which were to be changed into so many flowers: now violets, another time roses, then cornflowers, daisies, or forget-me-nots—in a word, all nature's blossoms were to form in me a cradle for the Holy Child.

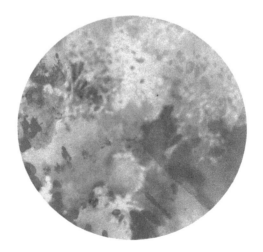

Strew flowers before Jesus

I ask only for Love. To love You, Jesus, is now my only desire. Great deeds are not for me; I cannot preach the Gospel or shed my blood. No matter! … I, a little child, stay close to the throne, and love You for all who are in the strife.

But how will I show my love, since love proves itself by deeds? Well! The little child will strew flowers . . . she will embrace the Divine Throne with their fragrance, she will sing Love's Canticle in silvery tones. Yes, my Beloved, it is thus my short life shall be spent in Thy sight. The only way I have of proving my love is to strew flowers before You—that is to say, I will let no tiny sacrifice pass, no look, no word. I wish to profit by the smallest actions, and to do them for Love

Roses must be gathered from amid thorns

I will sing always, even if my roses must be gathered from amid thorns; and the longer and sharper the thorns, the sweeter shall be my song.

Charity ought to betray itself in deeds

A holy nun of our community annoyed me in all that she did; the devil must have had something to do with it, and he it was undoubtedly who made me see in her so many disagreeable points. I did not want to yield to my natural antipathy, for I remembered that charity ought to betray itself in deeds, and not exist merely in the feelings, so I set myself to do for this sister all I should do for the one I loved most. Every time I met her I prayed for her, and offered to God her virtues and merits. I felt that this was very pleasing to Our Lord, for there is no artist who is not gratified when his works are praised, and the Divine Artist of souls is pleased when we do not stop at the exterior, but, penetrating to the inner sanctuary He has chosen, admire its beauty.

I did not rest satisfied with praying for this Sister, who gave me such occasions for self-mastery; I tried to render her as many services as I could, and when tempted to answer her sharply, I made haste to smile and change the subject, for the *Imitation* says: "It is better to leave everyone to his way of thinking than to give way to argument."

And sometimes when the temptation was very severe, I would run like a deserter from the battlefield if I could do so without letting the Sister guess my inward struggle.

One day she said to me with a beaming face: "My dear Soeur Thérèse, tell me what attraction you find in me, for whenever we meet, you greet me with such a sweet smile." Ah! What attracted me was Jesus hidden in the depths of her soul: Jesus who makes sweet even that which is most bitter.

True love feeds on sacrifice.

Always see the good side of things

There are people who make the worst of everything. As for me, I do just the contrary. I always see the good side of things, and even if my portion be suffering, without a glimmer of solace, well, I make it my joy.

Show charity to others

Yes, I know when I show charity to others, it is simply Jesus acting in me, and the more closely I am united to Him, the more dearly I love my Sisters. If I wish to increase this love in my heart, and the devil tries to bring before me the faults of a Sister, I am quick to look for her virtues, her good motives; I call to mind that though I may have seen her fall once, no doubt she has gained many victories over herself, which in her humility she conceals. It is even possible that what seems to me a fault, may very likely, on account of her good intention, be an act of virtue.

In the heart of the Church, be love

Charity provided me with the key to my vocation. I understood that since the Church is a body composed of different members, the noblest and most important of all the organs would not be wanting. I knew that the Church has a heart, that this heart burns with love, and that it is love alone which gives life to its members. I knew that if this love were extinguished, the Apostles would no longer preach the Gospel, and the Martyrs would refuse to shed their blood. I understood that love embraces all vocations, that it is all things, and that it reaches out through all the ages, and to the uttermost limits of the earth, because it is eternal.

Then, beside myself with joy, I cried out: "O Jesus, my Love, at last I have found my vocation. My vocation is love! Yes, I have found my place in the bosom of the Church, and this place, O my God, You have Yourself given to me: in the heart of the Church, my Mother, I will be LOVE! … Thus I shall be all things: thus will my dream be realised…."

Rely upon Jesus alone

Do not let your weakness make you unhappy. When, in the morning, we feel no courage or strength for the practice of virtue, it is really a grace: it is the time to "lay the axe to the root of the tree," relying upon Jesus alone.… He helps us without seeming to do so…

Love can do all things. The most impossible tasks seem to it easy and sweet. You know well that Our Lord does not look so much at the greatness of our actions, nor even at their difficulty, as at the love with which we do them. What, then, have we to fear?

Find joy in imperfection

One day during prayer, it was brought home to me that…as I belonged to Our Lord and was His little plaything to console and please Him, it was for me to do His Will, not for Him to do mine.

At the beginning of my spiritual life, about the age of fourteen, I used to ask myself how, in days to come, I should more clearly understand the true meaning of perfection. I imagined I then understood it completely, but I soon came to realize that the more one advances along this path the farther one seems from the goal, and now I am resigned to be always imperfect, and I even find joy therein.

Choose everything

One day [my sister] Léonie…brought us a basket filled with clothes, pretty pieces of stuff, and other trifles on which her doll was laid: "Here, dears," she said, "choose whatever you like." Céline looked at it, and took a woollen ball. After thinking about it for a minute, I put out my hand saying: "I choose everything," and I carried off both doll and basket without more ado.

This childish incident was a forecast of my whole life. Later, when the way of perfection was opened before me, I realized that in order to become a Saint one must suffer much, always seek the most perfect path, and forget oneself. I also understood that there are many degrees of holiness, that each soul is free to respond to the calls of Our Lord, to do much or little for His Love—in a word, to choose among the sacrifices He asks. And as in the days of my childhood, I cried out: "My God, I choose everything, I will not be a Saint by halves, I am not afraid of suffering for You, I only fear one thing, and that is to do my own will. Accept the offering of my will, for I choose all that You desire."

Acknowledgments and Citations

The quote from Father James Martin, S.J., is from *My Life with the Saints* (Chicago: Loyola Press), 2006, p. 40.

Readers interested in reading *Story of a Soul* in its entirety are encouraged to seek out *Story of a Soul: The Autobiography of St. Thérèse of Lisieux*, Third Edition by John Clarke (ICS Publications), widely recognized as the best translation.

The words of St. Thérèse in this book are taken from *Story of a Soul (l'Histoire d'une Ame): The Autobiography of St. Therese of Lisieux*, an electronic edition produced by Christian Classics Ethereal Library (Grand Rapids, Michigan) and freely available online at http://www.ccel.org/ccel/therese. That edition is taken from *Soeur Thérèse of Lisieux*, edited by Rev. T.N. Taylor (London: Burns, Oates & Washbourne, 1912; 8th ed., 1922). Some of the excerpts found in this book have been slightly altered from the CCEL edition for the sake of readability.

The following citations refer to printed page numbers in the CCEL edition.

"accomplish the most heroic deeds": page 119
"I would be a light unto souls…": 119-120
Sing of God's goodness: 16-17
Acknowledge that all comes from God: 135
Bind yourself more closely to Jesus: 215
Open the Holy Gospels: 116
To love God alone: page 115
I lift up my heart to God in trust and love: 116-117
Getting to Heaven by a little way: 90
Remain always very little: 144
Await everything from the goodness of God: 145
"My way is the way of spiritual…": 137
"The nearer one approaches God…": 73
God will carry you: 144
Prayer is an uplifting of the heart: 107
Sacrifices and acts of love: 40
Strew flowers before Jesus: 122
Roses must be gathered from amid thorns: 122
Charity ought to betray itself in deeds: 100
"True love feeds on sacrifice": 104
Always see the good side of things: 163
Show charity to others: 97
In the heart of the Church, be love: 121
Rely upon Jesus alone: 170
Find joy in imperfection: 77
Choose everything: 21

CPSIA information can be obtained
at www.ICGtesting.com
Printed in the USA
BVHW021216060819
555200BV00016B/206/P

9 781944 008116